STRIDE
PARTICIPANT BOOK

MIKE SCHREINER
KEN WILLARD

STRIDE
PARTICIPANT BOOK

CREATING A
DISCIPLESHIP PATHWAY
FOR YOUR LIFE

Abingdon Press™

Nashville

STRIDE PARTICIPANT BOOK:
CREATING A DISCIPLESHIP PATHWAY FOR YOUR LIFE

Copyright © 2018 by Abingdon Press

This book is printed on acid-free paper.

978-1-5018-7625-7

18 19 20 21 22 23 24 25 26 27—10 9 8 7 6 5 4 3 2 1
MANUFACTURED IN THE UNITED STATES OF AMERICA

CONTENTS

INTRODUCTION

Imagine a forty-five-year old man sitting with his oversized physique stuffed into a toddler's high chair. With a bib snapped around his neck, he's banging his fists on the table and crying, "Feed me. Feed me." Sadly, this scene plays out each weekend in thousands of churches across the nation. It's a reminder that, somewhere along the line, pastors failed to instruct and equip disciples to stop relying on the local church to spoon-feed them every bite, to take responsibility for their own spiritual journey, and to mature into a self-feeder.

In our book *Stride*, we talked about the importance of the local church to develop a Clear Path of Discipleship. This path clearly identifies a series of next steps a person would take in the context of that particular expression of the body of Christ. Each step is designed to help the person grow into the image of Jesus. As important as it is for the local church to develop and utilize that Clear Path of Discipleship, it is equally essential for each believer to have her or his own path of personal development. That is what this study offers—an intentional, systematic process for helping you identify where you are currently on your spiritual journey, and how to leverage eight specific spiritual disciplines to become the person God has created you to be.

Consider this word of advice as you work your way through this study. Pay attention to the spiritual disciplines you have already embraced the most. Your strengths tell you a lot about your personal spiritual wiring and how you most naturally connect with God in ways that bring you joy. Do not forsake those areas of strength in order to direct all your attention to areas in which you have taken less ground. Pour into your strengths even more. Then, as your spiritual muscles get stronger, identify one or two areas of opportunity and commit to taking a next step while continuing to do better at what you do best.

Chapter 1

DISCIPLESHIP OVERVIEW

No discipline is fun while it lasts, but it seems painful at the time. Later, however, it yields the peaceful fruit of righteousness for those who have been trained by it.

– Hebrews 12:11

Everyone who competes practices self-discipline in everything. The runners do this to get a crown of leaves that shrivel up and die, but we do it to receive a crown that never dies.

– 1 Corinthians 9:25

Train yourself for a holy life! While physical training has some value, training in holy living is useful for everything. It has promise for this life now and the life to come.

– 1 Timothy 4:7b-8

The 2004 Olympic Games were held in Athens, Greece. During those games, twenty-three-year-old American Matthew Emmons competed in several of the shooting competitions. Prior to the prone position event, he discovered that his rifle had been severely sabotaged and had to borrow a rifle from one of his teammates. Emmons won a gold medal in the event. Having won junior world records and several World Cup shooting events, he was considered one of the best competitors in the shooting events. After his first nine shots in the standing event, his lowest score was a 9.3, and with one

1

shot left to take he had what appeared to be an insurmountable lead of three points. All Emmons needed on the last shot was to get close to the bull's-eye to win a second gold medal. He fired, and the bullet struck just outside the bull's-eye. However, no score appeared on the board. After a few moments, an official informed the audience that Emmons had hit the wrong target. A "cross fire" had occurred. Instead of a gold medal, Emmons completely dropped off the Olympic platform and into eighth place.

Has anything like that ever happened to you? Have you ever been so focused on one thing only to discover that you are focusing on the wrong target? This happens to some of us when we focus all of our time and energy into our work, often with the good intentions of providing for our family, but only to discover that while we were immersed in our work, our family drifted apart.

Spiritual disciplines are practices that help us grow as disciples. While we all have the same target, growing into the likeness of Christ, we are all at different places on that journey. For many of us, that target of growing to be like Jesus can seem overwhelming. Our recommendation is to keep the correct target in mind but to focus first on just the next step.

Consider the navigation system on your phone. When you need directions to a destination, you type in the address. But all that is useless unless your phone has its GPS turned on and is able to determine your current location. You'll never get to where you want to go without identifying where you currently are. Once that happens, however, the entire focus becomes the first step, then the next turn. In other words, one step at a time. Keep taking those steps, and you'll arrive at your destination. The same is true with your spiritual journey.

Let's make this personal. Below is a graphic image representing our spiritual journey to grow closer to Jesus. First, notice that it is not a linear path. Growing as a disciple is never as easy as 1-2-3 and you're done. Around the circle, there are eight spiritual disciplines listed. This is not to say that these are the only spiritual disciplines, or even that these are the most important, only that these eight tend to be very important practices for our journey. You may want to add additional disciplines later, once you feel strong in these. If the center of the image is Jesus, then you may want to consider the outer part of the circle the point in your life when you started your spiritual journey.

Before you go any further, here are three important things to remember. First, wherever you are in each of the spiritual disciplines, that is okay. God will meet you right there. Where we are today is just the starting point of our journey, not the end. Second, this is not a competition. We need to stay focused on the destination, not where other people are on their journey. As long as we are still on this side of heaven, we all have steps to take. And third, what is most important is our next step. Even when we find ourselves lost, our GPS can get us back on the right route. Taking a wrong turn, or even stopping for a while, is not the end. The same is true for our spiritual journey.

Take a minute now to indicate where you feel you are today in each of the eight spiritual disciplines by placing a mark on the self-reflection image below.

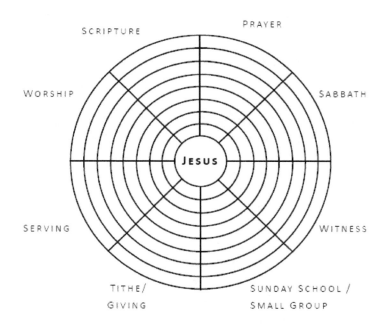

If our target is to grow into completely committed followers of Jesus Christ, how is that going? Let's look at four key elements to ensure we are focused on the correct target.

1. **Clarify Priorities.** Look back on your day yesterday, last week, last month. In most cases, where you spent your time will show your priorities. Take a minute now and write down the priorities in your life in the space below.

I once thought these things were valuable, but now I consider them worthless because of what Christ has done. Yes, everything else is worthless when compared with the infinite value of knowing Christ Jesus my Lord. For his sake I have discarded everything else, counting it all as garbage, so that I could gain Christ.

– Philippians 3:7-8, NLT

2. **Craft a Plan**. Look back at the spiritual discipline of self-reflection. Choose one area where you would like to take a step in this current season of life. In the space below, write down one action you can take to help you take the next step in that spiritual discipline.

Get your outside work done; make preparations in the field; then you can build your house.

– Proverbs 24:27

3. Consult Some Partners. We were not meant to take this journey alone. Accountability is born when two or more people know about a commitment. As you feel comfortable, consider sharing your plan with your group. (If you do not feel comfortable sharing with the whole group, please share your plan with at least one other person who can follow up with you on this journey.)

As iron sharpens iron, so one person sharpens another.

– Proverbs 27:17, NIV

4. Commence Practice. What action will you commit to taking between now and our next meeting? The emphasis should not be on going from one to one hundred in a week, but on moving from one to two. Just take the next small step. In the space below write your action step.

In his book *Celebration of Discipline*, Richard J. Foster says, "We must always remember that the path does not produce the change; it only places us where the change can occur." This is good reminder for all of us. Our personal discipleship pathway is an important tool for the journey. But it will not do the work for us. We must take action ourselves in order to grow into the disciple Jesus is calling us to be. The good news is that we are never on this journey alone. God's Spirit has been with us all along and will continue to be with us every step of the way. Our church and our group are also with us to provide encouragement, resources, and accountability as we journey together.

During the next few sessions, we will take a closer look at each of the eight spiritual disciplines mentioned above and some ways each of us can grow in those practices. We will end with an excerpt from *Mere Christianity* by C. S. Lewis. Reflect on how the image he describes applies to your spiritual journey.

> Imagine yourself as a living house. God comes in to rebuild that house. At first, perhaps, you can understand what He is doing. He is getting the drains right and stopping the leaks in the roof and so on; you knew that those jobs needed doing and so you are not surprised. But presently He starts knocking the house about in a way that hurts abominably and does not seem to make any sense. What on earth is He up to? The explanation is that He is building quite a different house from the one you thought of—throwing out a new wing here, putting on an extra floor there, running up towers, making courtyards. You thought you were being made into a decent little cottage; but He is building a palace. He intends to come and live in it Himself.

Group Discussion Questions

1. What has been your understanding of discipleship before reading this chapter?

2. Looking back, what has helped you the most to take a step on your spiritual journey?

3. In which of the eight spiritual disciplines do you feel strongest at this stage of your journey?

4.   How can this group best help you on your journey?

5.   Which part of our session today spoke to you the most? Why?

6.   How have you experienced God in your life this week?

Chapter 2
SPIRITUAL DISCIPLINE
OF SCRIPTURE

Every scripture is inspired by God and is useful for teaching, for showing mistakes, for correcting, and for training character, so that the person who belongs to God can be equipped to do everything that is good.

– 2 Timothy 3:16-17

Your word is so pleasing to my taste buds—it's sweeter than honey in my mouth!

– Psalm 119:103

Don't fool yourself into thinking that you are a listener when you are anything but, letting the Word go in one ear and out the other. Act *on what you hear! Those who hear and don't act are like those who glance in the mirror, walk away, and two minutes later have no idea who they are, what they look like.*

– James 1:22-24, MSG

Have you ever run out of gas? It's a terrible feeling. You're driving down the road, most likely running late to get somewhere, and suddenly your car starts to sputter and stall. You look over at the gas gauge and see it is below the "E." You pull off the road and probably feel embarrassed, frustrated, and many more emotions. Those of us born before cell phones might recall putting a dollar or so in our cars and knowing that if we ran out of gas...our only option would be to thumb a ride (i.e., hitchhike) or walk to a station for help.

There are many different types of fuel. While most cars run on gasoline, more and more are being powered by electricity. There are different types of trains around the world that use steam, coal, and diesel for fuel. Even though airplanes are required to carry enough additional fuel to reach their destination, *plus* an alternate destination, *plus* forty-five minutes, there have been cases of planes crashing due to running out of fuel. In 2016, a Colombian plane carrying a Brazilian football team crashed because it ran out of fuel as it tried to land.

Our human body also requires fuel. The main sources of fuel for our bodies are food, water, and air. While most of us could live for many days without food, we would only survive a few days without water, and only a matter of minutes without air.

So what fuels your life? And how is it working? Are you putting in the right kind of fuel that is getting you where you need to be? Or do you often find yourself frustrated and empty, or maybe just running on fumes?

As Christians, our fuel comes from reading and reflecting on scripture. This is God's word. It is how he speaks to us. If we want to know God better, understand his plans for our lives, and grow as a disciple of Jesus, it only makes sense that we spend time listening to him and hearing what he has to say about the things of life, about what's important to him.

Jesus said that knowing scripture was critical—even more important than food. After he'd been fasting from food for forty days, when the Enemy tempted him to turn stones to bread, Jesus replied, *"It's written, People won't live only by bread, but by every word spoken by God"* (Matthew 4:4). Jesus was saying that the word of God was more important to fuel his life than even physical food. And if that holds true for Jesus, God's Son, then how much more for ordinary people like all of us?

God gives us his word as a gracious gift of life. The Bible is a gift to us. It contains everything we need to know for our salvation, and everything we need to know about God and his purpose for creating us and giving us life. It gives us the direction we need, but it also gives us the fuel we need to live it out.

Look at what Moses told the Israelites long ago about the word of God. After God had given him the Ten Commandments, Moses passed them on to the people and said, *"Set your mind on all these words I'm testifying against you right now, because you must command your children to perform carefully all the words of this Instruction. This is no trivial matter for you—this is your very life!"* (Deuteronomy 32:46-47).

It is imperative to know that God doesn't give us his word to burden us or oppress us. It is not to confine or condemn us. It is designed to guide us away from places that lead to pain and suffering and deep regret . . . and lead us to the places where God can bless us. God's word is a gracious gift of life!

But here is the danger. Like so many things that God gives us as a blessing, the Evil One twists and turns, distorts and manipulates. And nowhere is this more true than when it comes to the Bible. The Enemy uses God's word to produce guilt and shame.

We have been told for years how we should read our Bibles. Most of us know that. It is not a big surprise. And yet, when we hear stories of people who actually do it, it is like they are a spiritual giant who gets up at 5:00 a.m. and spends an hour or two each day reading, journaling, and praying. It feels like there is a huge price we have to be willing to pay on the front end, so many of us do not ever even start.

But then some of us jump in and get started. We tell ourselves that we can do it, that the Bible is not that big—sixty-six books divided into 1,189 chapters. In fact, we will do it in a year—365 days from Genesis through Revelation—which figures out to a little more than three chapters a day. So we go out and buy one of those, "One-Year, Guilt-Trip Reading Plans" (not the real name). Have you ever done that? And we start off great. But then about a month or so in, we are in the middle of Leviticus learning about all the details of the precious stones and metallic ores used for building the Tent of Meeting, and we hit a wall. We get behind one day and work hard the next day to get up a little earlier and read twice as much. But then something happens, and one day behind becomes a week, and then one week becomes two. Now we are racing to get our reading in each day. We are cranky and feel bad because we are not able to spend time becoming more like Jesus.

So here is what happens. This book, given to us by God to bless us and protect us, actually becomes a source of guilt and shame. No longer do we pick it up and read it to give us life. It sits on our bookshelf or on our bedside table, and every time we look at it, it scolds us for being such a failure.

This is tragic. It is tragic because nowhere in the Bible does God say we need to read through it every 365 days. Not that there is anything wrong with that. It is great when we are in that season as a disciple. But not everyone can or will read the Bible completely each year. There is a better way, especially if we want to become closer to God, to have that personal relationship. A way for us to tap into the truth in this book and use it to fuel the rest of our life. The key is to develop a practice designed less around getting through the word of God and more around getting the word of God through us.

Fueling Up on God's Word

1. Pray for Insight.

This first step is critical. We must slow down enough before we jump into reading to ask God to be with us. Psalm 46:10 says, *"Be still, and know that I am God"* (NIV). Invite him to be part of your reading time. Tell him that you want to know him and his will for your life. Psalm 119:105 says, *"Your word is a lamp before my feet and a light for my journey."* Ask him to help you make the most of your time together, to reveal the things that you need to know for your direction, your path in life. A great prayer that you can pray is actually a verse from Psalm 119—a psalm, ironically that is all about God's word: *"Open my eyes so I can examine the wonders of your Instruction!"* (Psalm 119:18).

2. Read for Depth, Not Distance.

Many of us remember cramming for some type of test or final exam in school. In some cases, we were trying to read everything we should have been reading the past semester—all in one night. We were reading for distance. Reading for depth, on the other hand, is not being content to just skim over the surface of a lot of scripture, but to be willing to just sit and soak in a smaller amount. The idea being that the more we can soak in it, the more nuggets we are going to mine out.

In the book *The Spiritual Disciplines for the Christian Life*, author Don Whitney shares the illustration of holding a glass of room-temperature water. The water is not hot, because sometimes when you come to the Bible, you are not all hot and fired up. Sometimes you are just lukewarm. Imagine what would happen if we were to dip a tea bag in the water once. There would not really be any difference. But if we take the tea bag and just let it sit in the water a while—let it steep—after ten or fifteen minutes, a change is going to happen. The water will begin to take on the character of the tea—the color, the flavor, and the aroma. The glass of water is our soul. The bag of tea is just a piece of scripture. It is not a whole book—not even five or ten chapters. It is just one chapter. Or maybe just a part of a chapter. It might be just a paragraph. Or even one verse. But as we let it steep into our soul, as we read it slowly several times—maybe even in a few different versions or translations—we are going to begin to see a change. We are going to begin taking on the character and flavor and aroma of Christ.

3. Reflect and Record Insights.

This is a step that many people skip, but it is absolutely critical. Reflecting and recording insights is just sit with a notebook and pen and begin to write down the things that God brings to your mind as you are reading his word. This is the part of reading and reflecting on scripture where asking the right questions can be helpful. As you read, you can ask yourself things like:

- What does this scripture tell me about God?

- What does it tell me about humanity or the human condition?

- What's the main truth of this scripture?

- What are the key words, and why does God choose them?

Most importantly, ask God to show you how this applies to your life. What will you commit to change as a result of what God's word has shown you?

Psalm 119:58-59 says, *"I've sought your favor with all my heart; have mercy on me according to your word. I've considered my ways and turned my feet back to your laws."*

4. Remember Key Truth and Verses.

In marketing terms, what is the "sticky statement"? What is the ONE thing God wants you to know, remember, and apply to your life? What is the ONE thing you can take with you today that will guide and direct your steps, that will be a lamp to your feet and a light to your path, that will lead you to the destination God has prepared for you? This is the command that Joshua gave to his people when he said, *"Do not let this Book of the Law depart from your mouth; meditate on it day and night, so that you may be careful to do everything written in it. Then you will be prosperous and successful"* (Joshua 1:8, NIV).

In the movie *The Book of Eli*, Denzel Washington plays the main character, Eli, a person who has survived a nuclear holocaust. He is visited by God and guided to this sacred book—the only Bible that remains on earth—and is charged with the task of taking it to a certain destination. Would you be willing to take the Bible and carry it with you? Not leaving it on a shelf, but carrying it with you always as God's gift. It's fuel to give you life!

Group Discussion Questions

1. What is your current reading plan for the Bible?

2. Looking back, where have you struggled in reading the Bible?

3. How would you describe your current placement in the spiritual discipline of reading and reflecting on scripture? What might it look like to take a small step forward?

4. How can this group best help you on your journey?

5. Which part of our session today spoke to you the most? Why?

6. How have you experienced God in your life this week?

Chapter 3
SPIRITUAL DISCIPLINE OF PRAYER

The Three "B's" of Prayer

Be Still: *The Art of Slowing*

> *Be still and know that I am God.*
>
> *— Psalm 46:10, NIV*

Be Real: *The Gift of Authenticity*

> *When you search for me, yes, search for me with all your heart, you will find me.*
>
> *— Jeremiah 29:13*

Be Bold: *The Benefit of Grace*

> *Let us then approach God's throne of grace with confidence, so that we may receive mercy and find grace to help us in our time of need.*
>
> *— Hebrews 4:16, NIV*

> *When you pray, don't pour out a flood of empty words, as the Gentiles do. They think that by saying many words they'll be heard. Don't be like them, because your Father knows what you need before you ask. Pray like this:*

Our Father who is in heaven,
uphold the holiness of your name.
Bring in your kingdom
so that your will is done on earth as it's done in heaven.
Give us the bread we need for today.
Forgive us for the ways we have wronged you,
just as we also forgive those who have wronged us.
And don't lead us into temptation,
but rescue us from the evil one.

– Matthew 6:7-13

W̲hat is prayer? While there are many different definitions of prayer, a simple, everyday type of definition might be that prayer is just a conversation with God. In our last session, we focused on the spiritual discipline of reading the Bible. One way to connect these two sessions is to think of the Bible as God's part of the dialogue. Think of a really good conversation you had recently. Maybe it was with a family member or a best friend. Chances are the two of you did an almost equal amount of listening and talking during that conversation. That might be a good model to remember in our conversations with God: an equal amount of listening and talking.

The spiritual discipline of prayer can be a challenge to many Christians. Some people struggle with how to pray. Others find it too intimidating to bother God with what they feel are items too small for an all-powerful God. Maybe you have heard pastors or others who seem to have a direct connection to God, and who pray such wonderfully worded prayers that you find your prayers lacking in comparison. Like all of the sections in this study, wherever we find ourselves in the spiritual discipline of prayer today is perfect! God will meet us right there. Our challenge, as always, is to intentionally take a step of growth.

While all of the spiritual disciplines are important, the discipline of prayer can be seen as foundational. Prayer is the discipline upon which we build. Prayer should be a key link between God and us. Often, our prayers will usually reflect our understanding of God. Do we see the Almighty as the Creator of the Universe, or as some type of cosmic counselor? Like someone we go to, lie down on the couch, and share our thoughts and issues with? The size of our Savior might be an indication of the size of our faith and confidence. As our faith withers, so do our prayers. They become small and superficial. If our vision of God has become weak, now is the time to turn that around! We must recapture a vision of hope and confidence and trust, to remember that the One who created the sun and moon, and hung the stars in the sky also knitted us together in our mother's womb and continues to be with us and for us. God has a will and purpose for our lives that far exceeds a daily maintenance plan. He created us for goodness and greatness. We are here to partner with him and make visible the invisible, to bring the kingdom on earth as it is in heaven.

It begins with prayer—bold prayer that demands an audacious faith, mature prayers offered with a childlike faith, trusting in an all-knowing, all-present, all-powerful God to show himself strong in our lives. Let us lift our sights, lift our eyes unto the Lord. Stop settling for low-level living. Stop praying pathetic, scrawny, wimpy prayers. Instead, once again start praying powerful, wonder-filled prayers that expect the miraculous intervention of a God who is sick and tired of us keeping him stuck like a lump on a throne in heaven. Let us pray prayers that truly open us to God's divine intervention in ways that will immediately and permanently impact our lives.

Make no mistake, praying these kinds of prayers will change us. They will not only change the way we see God, but also the way we behave—the things we say and do, the way we spend our lives and invest our resources of time, talent, and treasure. Bold prayers not only affect the presence of God in our lives, but they affect us as well. And of course, we are the ones in need of change. Imagine this example: When is the last time you prayed for rain on a completely sunny day—one with nothing showing on the radar, and with a forecast of zero percent precipitation—AND you carried your umbrella with you to work?

There is a wonderful story in scripture where God's people took it one step further. Not only did they pray for rain, but they demonstrated even more faith than packing their umbrellas. In the book of 2 Kings, chapter three, we read about an interesting time when God met his people right where they were, and through miraculous provision, helped them take a step to the victory he had already prepared.

Let's set the scene. God's people had become two nations—Judah in the south, and Israel in the north. But despite the division, they were still a dominant Middle Eastern force. Surrounding nations had become their vassals, who were expected to pay tribute to the dominant country in exchange for not being destroyed. One such country was Moab, whose contract called for 100,000 lambs, and the wool from another 100,000 rams. But Moab rebelled and withheld their tribute, which precipitated action from Joram, the king of Israel. He calls on the king of Judah, Jehoshaphat, and the king of the neighboring nation of Edom, and the three of them, and their armies, march against Moab.

As they are going through the desert of Edom, the armies run out of water. They are too far in to turn back, and they are too far away from the next water supply to make it there. The men and their animals are going to die in the middle of the desert if something drastic doesn't happen. So they call on the prophet Elisha to see what God had to say about the matter. Had one of them sinned—or was God angry with one of the nations—and had brought them out in the desert to destroy them?

God wanted to teach them a lesson of a different sort—a lesson of faith. Namely, that they could trust him. In the coming battle against Moab, God would certainly be with them and guarantee their victory. And as a sign of that, God said he would provide water for their immediate need—but not with rain, not with precipitation of any kind. Instead, water would just miraculously appear, kind of like the manna he provided the Israelites with during the forty years they walked in the desert wilderness some four hundred years earlier.

> *[Elisha] said, "This is what the LORD says: This valley will be filled with pools. This is what the LORD says: You won't see any wind or rain, but that valley will be full of water. Then you'll be able to drink—you, your cattle, and your animals. This is easy for the LORD to do. He will also hand Moab over to you."*
> (2 Kings 3:16-18)

In this text we see two miracles: the miraculous provision of water, but then there is the miracle before the miracle—the miracle of faith. The soldiers laid down their weapons in the middle of a desert on a day when there wasn't a cloud in the sky—not even a one percent chance of rain for the next four months—and they took up their shovels and began to dig ditches!

Who knows. Maybe this was their only hope. They were at the end of their rope, and they had nothing to lose. God has been known to work miracles in such circumstances even today, when people are so far down that they only have two directions to go—sideways or up. When people have exhausted every human avenue, and finally—with what feels like the proverbial Hail Mary—turn to God in prayer.

What does "rain" look like for you in your ongoing struggle or situation? Is it your health? Is it healing for a broken relationship? Is it concerning employment or for financial provision? Are you tired of carrying guilt or grief or grudges? Maybe your search is spiritual—you desperately want to grow closer to God, to know that he is really there and he really cares. Our need for God to intervene, to meet us where we are, and to show himself strong in our lives are as numerous as we are individually different than anyone else in the world.

Maybe you have already been praying for "rain" for your situation. There is no easy answer to why the situation hasn't changed. As we reflect on these verses, we need to ask ourselves: Have we really asked God about the situation, about what he might want us to hear from him, learn from him, or do in response to the situation to prepare to receive his intervention or answer? In the book *Too Busy Not to Pray*, Bill Hybels says, "If the request is wrong, God says, 'No.' If the timing is wrong, God says, 'Slow.' If you are wrong, God says, 'Grow.' But if the request is right, the timing is right and you are right, God says, 'Go!'"

Sometimes, God expects us to place ourselves in a position to receive the miracle. We may have put in our order, but we haven't purposed ourselves to align with God's will for us. We've prayed, but we haven't prepared. In terms of the account from scripture, the truth God wants us to lay hold of is this: If I dig the ditch, then God will send the rain.

Too often, we limit ourselves by limiting God. Maybe it is a way to avoid taking any responsibility for our own actions. Maybe it is a way of buying into the Evil One's lie that we don't deserve deliverance from our sins or struggles. Or it could even be a way we insulate ourselves from being disappointed if our prayers aren't answered the way we've asked. Whatever the reason, it is a spiritual death loop we set up in our minds, a lie Satan speaks into our lives: that all things are NOT possible with God, and that whatever we find ourselves stuck in is like quicksand from which there is no escape—permanent and eventually deadly.

But there is a solution. And the solution lies within the very thing that God wants from us more than anything else—a relationship, time together, sharing our heart and listening for God's voice. The spiritual practice of prayer is the antidote to our low expectations for ourselves and God—but not just any prayers. Not just the "God is great, God is good, let us thank him for our food," or the "now I lay me down to sleep, I pray the Lord my soul to keep" prayers. Instead, the spiritual practice type of prayers that call for breakthrough, deliverance, transformation. BOLD prayers!

Here is the lesson God needs us to learn as we begin to pray in a new and bigger way: The first truth about BOLD prayer is that BOLD prayers demand audacious faith. Asking for rain means more than just packing our umbrella. It means a willingness to take up our shovel and dig the "ditch"—a reservoir where we can receive God and the grace and power and truth he wants to offer us.

- Audacity: boldness or daring, especially with confident or arrogant disregard for personal safety, conventional thought, or other restrictions.

- Faith: confidence or trust in a person or thing

The Bible says, in Hebrews 11:1: *"Now faith is confidence in what we hope for and assurance about what we do not see"* (NIV). In Hebrews 11:6 we read: *"Without faith it is impossible to please God"* (NIV).

In his book *Sun Stand Still*, Stephen Furtick holds both sides of the equation in tension. He says, "If you're not daring to believe God for the impossible, you're sleeping through some of the best parts of your Christian life." He says there is a direct connection between the greatness of God and our potential to do great things on his behalf. Further, "if the size of your vision for life isn't intimidating to you, there's a good chance it's insulting to God."

Audacious faith is not the modern-day invention of Stephen Furtick. Rather, it is the faith God asked for from his people since the beginning of time, throughout the Old Testament and New Testament. It is the faith of Jesus Christ—the faith he had in his Heavenly Father and the faith he called his disciples to possess. In Matthew 17:20, Jesus says, *"I assure you that if you have faith the size of a mustard seed, you could say to this mountain, 'Go from here to there,' and it will go. There will be nothing that you can't do."*

Of course, that is not a carte blanche promise. God is not a genie in a bottle who gives us three wishes, or a blank check we can use selfishly for something that directly opposes God's will. And yet, audacious faith invites us to know and trust that God cannot and will not be limited by human thoughts or conventional modes of operation; that he loves us and cares for us, and will send forth the resources of heaven to bring the rain he desires us to receive.

Here are three aspects of audacious faith for us to consider as we grow in the spiritual discipline of prayer:

1. Audacious Faith Believes God for the Unbelievable.

This is the kind of faith Mary demonstrated when the angel announced her immaculate conception. *"The angel replied, 'The Holy Spirit will come over you and the power of the Most High will overshadow you. Therefore, the one who is to be born will be holy. He will be called God's Son. Look, even in her old age, your relative Elizabeth has conceived a son. This woman who was labeled "unable to conceive" is now six months pregnant. Nothing is impossible for God.' Then Mary said, 'I am the Lord's servant. Let it be with me just as you have said.' Then the angel left her"* (Luke 1:35-38).

The Apostle Paul writes this promise in Ephesians 3:20—a verse we should commit to memory: *"God . . . is able to do far beyond all that we could ask or imagine by his power at work within us."* Faith is a gift from God. It comes to us by way of the Holy Spirit, who works within us. It is audacious faith that believes God for the unbelievable . . . that nothing is impossible for God.

2. Audacious Faith Asks God for the Unreasonable.

When all the medical tests have come back and the prognosis is bleak, audacious faith asks God for healing. When the divorce papers have already been filed, audacious faith asks God for reconciliation. When you have fallen to the same temptation a million times, audacious faith asks God for supernatural power to deliver you from that temptation.

Audacious faith asks God for the unfeasible, the highly unlikely, the "it's never happened like that before." Look at what Jesus had to say: *"Have faith in God! I assure you that whoever says to this mountain, 'Be lifted up and thrown into the sea'—and doesn't waver but believes that what is said will really happen—it will happen. Therefore I say to you, whatever you pray and ask for, believe that you will receive it, and it will be so for you"* (Mark 11:22-24).

3. Audacious Faith Acts with Uncompromised Obedience.

There is a wonderful story in scripture when the disciples were out in a boat on the Sea of Galilee and Jesus comes out to them, walking on the water. They are having trouble believing they are not seeing a ghost. Peter says, *"'Lord, if it's you, order me to come to you on the water.' And Jesus said, 'Come.' Then Peter got out of the boat and was walking on the water toward Jesus"* (Matthew 14:28-29).

That is the faith of a desert ditch-digger. It is audacious faith that believes what our Heavenly Father chronicled in the Bible. A God who is never weak or wimpy. A God who calls us to believe that miracles continue to be his specialty. And that he has at least one big one reserved for us. The only question is, are we willing to dig the ditch? Will we believe enough to act in such a way that we will receive God's "rain" even today?

Group Discussion Questions

1. What excites you about growing in the spiritual discipline of prayer?

2. Looking back, where have you struggled with prayer? When have you felt the most joy in prayer?

3. How would you describe your current placement in the spiritual discipline of prayer? What might it look like to take a small step forward?

4. How can this group best help you on your journey?

5. Which part of our session today spoke to you the most? Why?

6. How have you experienced God in your life this week?

Chapter 4
SPIRITUAL DISCIPLINE OF SERVING

Now you are coming to him as to a living stone. Even though this stone was rejected by humans, from God's perspective it is chosen, valuable. You yourselves are being built like living stones into a spiritual temple. You are being made into holy priesthood to offer up spiritual sacrifices that are acceptable to God through Jesus Christ.

— 1 Peter 2:4-5

But you are a chosen race, a royal priesthood, a holy nation, a people who are God's own possession. You have become this people so that you may speak of the wonderful acts of the one who called you out of darkness into his amazing light.

— 1 Peter 2:9

Instead, we are God's accomplishment, created in Christ Jesus to do good things. God planned for these good things to be the way that we live our lives.

— Ephesians 2:10

The great violinist Niccolò Paganini willed his wonderful violin to Genoa, Italy, the city where he was born. His only condition was that the violin could never be played. This turned out to be a very ill-fated condition, since the wood used on this instrument holds up best as long as it is handled and played frequently. What was once a beautiful and well-toned violin has now become a moldering relic, of no service to anyone.

God has created each of us for ministry. As we read in Ephesians 2:10 above, we were created to do good works. God has shaped us each uniquely to serve in his kingdom. Other versions of this verse from Ephesians say *"…which God prepared in advance for us to do."* How wonderful is that! The God of the universe shaped us distinctively and prepared specific ways for us to use our individual shape to serve others.

Have you ever given any thought into how God has uniquely shaped you? In the book *S.H.A.P.E.: Finding and Fulfilling Your Unique Purpose for Life*, author Erik Rees uses the acronym S.H.A.P.E. to stand for Spiritual Gifts, Heart, Abilities, Personality, and Experiences. Take a minute now to answer the following questions:

1. What are your spiritual gifts? If you are not certain, then consider what you enjoy doing that seems to help others. Where do you seem to be "in your element" around church?

2. What breaks your heart? Or maybe, what cause or concern do you really have a heart for?

3. What abilities has God given to you? What do you just seem to be good at doing?

4. How would you and others describe your personality?

5. What life experiences have you had that might be of benefit to others?

While this is not a substitute for reading Rees's book or taking a class on spiritual gifts, this should give you a good starting point for understanding how God has shaped you. All of those five elements above will point you toward where God is calling you to serve in his ministry. We are each created for ministry, and God has shaped us for that ministry.

What does it mean to be called into ministry? For most of us, when we hear about someone being called into ministry, we think of pastors, church staff, missionaries, and others who are ordained or at least working full-time in some form of church ministry. That is true. These people were called into ministry.

But guess what? So are all of us! Take another look at 1 Peter 2:9. Paul is saying that all of us are a "royal priesthood," thus we are all ministers. Yes, for some that will take the form of full-time church service. But for the vast majority of Christians, our ministry will look different. However—and this is important—we are ALL called into ministry, and ALL ministry is equally important to God and his kingdom.

A great companion verse to us being created and called into ministry is Ephesians 4:12 where we read, *"His purpose was to equip God's people for the work of serving and building up the body of Christ."* Each of has been equipped for serving and building up the body of Christ, which is the local church. One of the most common reasons people give about why they are not serving anywhere in the church is that they do not feel they have anything to offer. In some cases, a person will compare themselves to others and feel inadequate. In other cases, they see people serving and are not aware of any opening where they might use their gifts. This "voice" is not the voice of God's Spirit. Be careful. God has equipped you. God has a place for you in his church.

The local church you call home has something you need. It is a place where we can worship our creator with other believers, have our cup filled, encounter the Holy Spirit, connect with people to learn and grow into the image of Christ, and much more. The local church also needs each and every one of us. Without our S.H.A.P.E. at work in ministry, the body of Christ is incomplete and unable to fulfil its true potential. When we hold out, others miss out. Consider this your "tap on the shoulder." God wants you to partner with him to serve others.

With all the serving ministry options available in most churches, how do you figure out where to serve? Here are two ways to approach this question. First, how has God gifted you for ministry? Remember the S.H.A.P.E. activity? Your responses there should at least point you in the direction of your primary serving ministry. If you are not serving now, or if you have had some bad experiences and chose to take a season off, then you might ask the ministry leader if it would be possible to "try out" serving in their area, just to ensure the fit is correct. Here is a great way to tell if you are serving in an area where God has equipped you to serve: It will not feel like work. This is in no way "shopping around" to find a ministry you like. This is about matching up your gifts to the correct ministry. When this happens, everyone wins!

Once you have found your primary serving ministry, prayerfully consider serving in a secondary area. While having everyone serve in their areas of giftedness is every church's goal, until we reach that level, there are always going to be needs. Your secondary area of serving is where we put the white towel over our arm and joyfully fill in a gap to ensure everything that needs to be done in our church is done. For example, your church might not have anyone at the moment who is gifted in washing dishes. However, the dishes used during the potluck dinner will still need to be washed. A more important example might be when a local church does not have anyone identified and trained for the nursery, but there are still parents who expect and need to see a smiling face working there when they drop off their children.

Serving in our primary area should be filling our spirit. Serving in our secondary area might be draining at times. Both are needed for our churches to fulfill our mission.

While the word *volunteer* is used quite often in local churches, that is not the word used in the Bible. The word we find in the Bible is *servant*. Think about the difference between those two terms. How would you define *volunteer*? While volunteer is certainly a good word, and those who volunteer are good people, the level of commitment might be low. A volunteer might be someone who helps out when it is convenient to them. There is a need somewhere in the church and their calendar is open during that time, so they pitch in to help. Again, nothing wrong with that at all.

However, how would you define *servant*? Do you picture Jesus washing the dirty feet of his disciples? Where would you imagine the level of commitment to be for a servant? Usually very high. A servant is one who puts the needs of others above their own. They are serving because that is what God has created and called them to do. The work might be unrewarding, anonymous, and inconvenient. But they are there serving with joy and spreading that joy to everyone they encounter.

In the parable of the coins, Jesus tells the story of a man leaving on a trip and entrusting three of his servants with various amounts of coins. The first two took what the man gave them and multiplied it. *"His master replied, 'Well done! You are a good and faithful servant. You've been faithful over a little. I'll put you in charge of much. Come, celebrate with me"* (Matthew 23:25). Are we expecting God to greet us in heaven by saying, "Thanks for volunteering," or do we want to hear God say, "Well done, good and faithful servant"?

The spiritual discipline of serving is important to our local churches. It is also very important to each person wanting to grow into the image of Christ Jesus. Have you ever heard some share a story of a mission trip they just completed? No matter if the trip was overseas, across the country, or within the state, at some point in the story we often hear the person say some version of "I got so much more out of the experience than I ever expected!" They were serving God's kingdom. While washing the windows or working in the children's area might not seem the same as going on a mission trip, it is all service to God. The spiritual growth opportunity is there in both options.

What voice are you hearing now about serving? Do you hear guilt? Do you hear excuses? That is not God's voice speaking to you. God's Spirit will encourage and fill you with joy. However, as soon as you consider taking a next step in this (and all other spiritual disciplines), Satan will give you excuses to stay the same. You may hear that serving is inconvenient, it will make you feel uncomfortable, or that you are inadequate. Remember, God doesn't excuse anybody because God has gifted everyone. Using God's gifts honors God, blesses others, and grows us into the image of Jesus.

There are different spiritual gifts but the same Spirit; and there are different ministries and the same Lord; and there are different activities but the same God who produces all of them in everyone.

– 1 Corinthians 12:4-6

Group Discussion Questions

1. Looking back, where have you served in a local church where you felt you were using your S.H.A.P.E.? When have you felt the most joy in serving?

2. What do you see as your primary area of serving? What ministry area is now, or might become, your secondary area of serving?

3. Over the years, what has been your main obstacle with serving in your local church?

4. How can this group best help you on your journey?

5. Which part of our session today spoke to you the most? Why?

6. How have you experienced God in your life this week?

Chapter 5
SPIRITUAL DISCIPLINE
OF GENEROSITY

All tenth-part gifts from the land, whether of seed from the ground or fruit from the trees, belong to the LORD; they are holy to the LORD.

– Leviticus 27:30

The money lover isn't satisfied with money; neither is the lover of wealth satisfied with income. This too is pointless.

– Ecclesiastes 5:10

What I mean is this: the one who sows a small number of seeds will also reap a small crop, and the one who sows a generous amount of seeds will also reap a generous crop.

– 2 Corinthians 9:6

Bring the whole tenth-part to the storage house so there might be food in my house. Please test me in this, says the LORD of heavenly forces. See whether I do not open all the windows of the heavens for you and empty out a blessing until there is enough.

– Malachi 3:10

"Earn all you can, give all you can, save all you can."

– John Wesley, founder of the Methodist movement

When we go to the doctor for an annual checkup, the doctor will often poke, prod, and press various places on our body while asking, "Does this hurt?" If we cry out in pain, usually one of two things has happened. Either the doctor has pushed too hard, without the correct amount of pressure, or there is something wrong and the doctor will need to run more tests. The same thing happens with some Christians when they hear a message on giving. Some people in the congregation will cry out in pain, upset with the message and the pastor. Either the pastor has pushed too hard, or more likely, there is something wrong in the person's spiritual life. In both cases, we are in need of the Great Physician because there should not be pain when we hear a message on money.

How about you? How do you feel when the pastor preaches on money? Too often we hear the words *stewardship* or *generosity* or *giving* and tune out the rest of the message. One of the dangers when this happens is that we are potentially missing out on a very important spiritual discipline. Our Father in heaven does not want us to miss out on all great gifts he has for us. This means becoming complete Christians, not holding back on this, or any, spiritual discipline.

God makes this promise to us throughout scripture—that he will bless us when we bring our firstfruits, the first portion of all we earn, as an offering to him. It is a promise that he even invites us to test him on, because he knows how much power money tends to have in our lives, how we tend to turn lots of things over to God before our finances. It is a promise many people have discovered in their own lives—one that helps them get out of debt and live with peace and assurance in God's provision. Chances are there are people in your own life, maybe in your church or group, who have seen God keep this promise. Time after time, people seem to be absolutely amazed that when they take God at his word—and take a true step of faith—that he will keep his promise and bless them.

Our heavenly Father wants the very best for us, his children. We need to move from "what God wants *from me*" to "what God wants *for me*."

- From Duty to Desire

- From Scarcity to Generosity

- From Debt to Freedom

- From Fear to Faith

Does God want obedience from us? Absolutely! Does God want faith and trust? Nothing is more important to him! Why? Because those things ultimately bring blessings into our lives. And that is what God wants! It is why he sent his one and only Son—to give us what we could not earn for ourselves: the gift of eternal life. And it is why he sent his Holy Spirit—to guide us into the fullness of his truth and grace, to give us the power to move from conventional wisdom to godly truth. And the fruit of all this is listed by the Apostle Paul in Galatians 5:22-23: *"But the fruit of the Spirit is love, joy, peace, patience, kindness, goodness, faithfulness, gentleness, and self-control."* God is committed to transform our obedience, trust, and faith into a harvest of blessings, things so awesome and amazing that money cannot even buy them.

Your church and your pastor want the best for you and your family. They would be less than trustworthy if they told you only the things you wanted to hear, especially if they did not share the truths and promises of scripture that would bring blessings into your life. Hopefully you have heard many times the truth that we are saved by the gift of God's grace instead of our works, so we will not spend our lives trying to prove our worth to God by our works. We have the assurance of our salvation. We should not feel like every sin disqualifies our eternity in heaven and most of all that we know how good God is to bless us with this gift.

Thus, preaching on money is a pastoral care issue. It is about bringing us God's blessing and saving us from the temptation of the Evil One, who loves when we prioritize anything—including money—above God. As the Apostle Paul writes in 1 Timothy 6:10: *"The love of money is the root of all kinds of evil. Some have wandered away from the faith and have impaled themselves with a lot of pain because they made money their goal."*

In 2 Corinthians, Paul is writing to the church in Corinth prior to his visit. In the ninth chapter of this book, Paul is teaching the Christians about the grace of giving and encouraging them to complete the collection for poor Christians living in Jerusalem. He writes,

What I mean is this: the one who sows a small number of seeds will also reap a small crop, and the one who sows a generous amount of seeds will also reap a generous crop. Everyone should give whatever they have decided in their heart. They shouldn't give with hesitation or because of pressure. God loves a cheerful giver. God has the power to provide you with more than enough of every kind of grace. That way, you will have everything you need always and in everything to provide more than enough for every kind of good work. As it is written, He scattered everywhere; he gave to the needy; his righteousness remains forever. The one who supplies seed for planting and bread for eating will supply and multiply your seed and will increase your crop, which is righteousness. You will be made rich in every way so that you can be generous in every way. Such generosity produces thanksgiving to God through us. (2 Corinthians 9:6-11)

There is a lot of wisdom packed into those few verses! Paul is writing to people in order to teach them that giving is not about the law, but about being cheerful and knowing that God will provide. Many of us are living in one of the richest countries in the world. We may not consider ourselves rich, but when compared to the majority of people in the world, we are. So we need to go back now and read those last two sentences. We have been made rich *so that* we can be generous in every way. God will truly bless us when we have demonstrated faith in him, when our life, money, and possessions are all offered back to him, and we are willing to use our time, talent, and treasure to bless others. This is the difference between the gospel preached in most of our churches and the Prosperity Gospel you often hear on TV. Those preachers tell you that God wants to bless you so you can keep elevating your level of living. But God does not promise that. He promises to meet our needs; and then to bless us abundantly so we can raise our level of giving. Why? To get in on what he is doing! To realize that life's greatest blessings are when we use what we have been blessed with to bless others.

God will provide for our needs. Paul says God will bless us *"abundantly, so that in all things at all times, having all that you need, you will abound in every good work"* (2 Corinthians 9:8, NIV). Just like the law of sowing and reaping he repeatedly mentions, this is one of Paul's fundamental teachings of faith. Here is what he writes in Philippians 4:19: *"My God will meet your every need out of his riches in the glory that is found in Christ Jesus."*

Here are two challenges for you on this journey of giving:

First, move from closed to open. The moment a pastor or anyone at church starts talking about money, so many people tune out, check out, or build walls, which is exactly what the Enemy wants you to do. He wants to rob you of the blessing God has for you. So the first challenge is to simply stay open—to prayerfully listen to what God's Spirit is saying to you about this very important area of your spiritual life. One way to go deeper would be to read the book *The Genius of Generosity* by Chip Ingram.

Consider John Wesley, the founder of Methodism, who lived in the late 1700s. He had been a pastor for several years. He knew God. He knew God's word. But he records the following in his journal as the defining moment in his life.

> In the evening I went very unwillingly to a society in Aldersgate Street, where one was reading Luther's preface to the Epistle to the Romans. About a quarter before nine, while he was describing the change which God works in the heart through faith in Christ, I felt my heart strangely warmed. I felt I did trust in Christ, Christ alone, for salvation; and an assurance was given me that He had taken away my sins, even mine, and saved me from the law of sin and death.

No one is asking us to give unwillingly. As we saw, scripture teaches the direct opposite of this—that we are to give cheerfully. We just need to move from being closed to being open.

The second challenge is to prayerfully consider taking the next step on our generosity journey. Imagine a giving pathway for all Christians. Five of the main steps might be:

- **Initial**—I have never given to my church before now. A person at this stage may just place twenty dollars in the offering plate. What a wonderful start to their journey!

- **Consistent**—I give to my church regularly, but not based on a percentage of my income. Instead of only giving when they are at a worship service and not putting any thought, or prayer, into the giving, a person at this level is giving a set dollar amount.

- **Percentage**—I give a percentage to my church, just not a full ten percent tithe. A person at this stage has moved from focusing on a dollar amount to beginning to see their income as all coming from God and wanting to give a percentage of that back.

- **Priority**—I faithfully give ten percent of my income (tithe) to my church. A person at this stage is likely giving God what is right, not what is left. They understand and embrace the "firstfruits" element of giving.

- **Extravagant**—I give beyond my tithe. A person at this stage tends to focus on what to keep, not what to give.

In many churches, the pastor or someone will say something like, "It is time to take up our tithes, gifts, and offerings" before the ushers pass around the offering plates. Have you ever given any thought to those words? Many Christians think tithes, gifts and offerings are all the same thing. As you are considering a next step on your giving journey, you may also want to reflect on what these terms really mean:

- **Tithe**—a tenth of all we have received from God. The firstfruits. [See Genesis 28, Leviticus 27, 2 Chronicles 31:5-6, Proverbs 3:9-10.]

- **Gifts (almsgiving)**—giving to the poor, humanitarian interests, or benevolent concerns. Has been expanded to giving to a specific ministry or area and not to a church's general ministry fund.

- **Offering (freewill offering)**—originally seen as amounts in addition to the tithe. Now often used as any money given to the church during a worship service. Scripture is clear that offering is distinct from our tithe. [See Malachi 3, Deuteronomy 12:5-6.]

Wherever we are on our spiritual journey of giving, God will meet us right there and be with us as we take our next steps. Financial giving is a very personal and private area for many Christians. Hearing a message on stewardship or generosity can make us feel uncomfortable, like when our doctor pokes at our body and causes pain. Our heavenly Father wants only the best for us, which is why he wants us to put our trust in him and test him, so that he can open the floodgates of heaven and pour down blessings upon us!

Group Discussion Questions

1. Where have you experienced God's provision in your life? Where have you seen the Fruits of the Spirit in times where you really placed your total trust in God?

2. Over the years, what has been your main obstacle with giving to God through your local church?

3. What do you see as your next step on the giving pathway? What excites you about that step?

4. How can this group best help you on your journey?

5. Which part of our session today spoke to you the most? Why?

6. How have you experienced God in your life this week?

Chapter 6
SPIRITUAL DISCIPLINE OF WORSHIP

All the Israelites were watching when the fire fell. As the LORD's glory filled the temple, they knelt down on the pavement with their faces to the ground, worshipping and giving thanks to the LORD, saying, "Yes, God is good! Yes, God's faithful love lasts forever!"

– 2 Chronicles 7:3

Come, let's sing out loud to the Lord!
Let's raise a joyful shout to the rock of our salvation!
Let's come before him with thanks!
Let's shout songs of joy to him!
The Lord is a great God,
the great king over all other gods.
The earth's depths are in his hands;
the mountain heights belong to him;
the sea, which he made, is his
along with the dry ground,
which his own hands formed.
Come, let's worship and bow down!
Let's kneel before the Lord, our maker!
He is our God,
and we are the people of his pasture,
the sheep in his hands.

– Psalm 95:1-7

In his 1958 book *Reflections on the Psalms*, author and theologian C. S. Lewis said,

> I think we delight to praise what we enjoy because the praise not merely expresses but completes the enjoyment; it is its appointed consummation. It is not out of compliment that lovers keep on telling one another how beautiful they are; the delight is incomplete till it is expressed. It is frustrating to have discovered a new author and not to be able to tell anyone how good he is; to come suddenly, at the turn of the road, upon some mountain valley of unexpected grandeur and then to have to keep silent because the people with you care for it no more than for a tin can in the ditch; to hear a good joke and find no one to share it with. . . . The Scotch catechism says that man's chief end is "to glorify God and enjoy Him forever." But we shall then know that these are the same thing. Fully to enjoy is to glorify. In commanding us to glorify Him, God is inviting us to enjoy Him.

Churches, and Christians, use the word *worship* all the time. Sometimes it is used to describe a time of music, and other times it is used to describe a weekly activity. But worship is more than just a service we attend for an hour or so each weekend. It's more than just the part of the service where we sing words of praise to God.

Worship is a posture and practice we are designed to do each and every day, because it is about being connected in relationship with God. Reflect on Christmas. Christmas is all about the incredible, almost inconceivable and miraculous gift of the incarnation: God stepping out of heaven and putting on human flesh so that, ultimately, he would give his life on the cross as an offering to pay the price for our sin. Worship is the truest response to that original and still greatest Christmas gift!

Consider that on the night Jesus was born:

- A great company of angels filled the sky and burst out in **worship**, singing, *"Glory to God in heaven, and on earth peace among those whom he favors"* (Luke 2:14).

- Shepherds in nearby fields left their flocks and traveled into town, to the stable, to lay eyes on this Savior. They returned **praising** and **glorifying** God for all they had witnessed.

- Even those hundreds of miles away began preparing to **worship** this newborn king. Magi/Wise Men from the East, who were probably astrologers, saw a new star in the sky—a star connected to a prophecy about the birth of the Jewish Messiah. So, they loaded up their camels, brought gifts, and stayed the course for somewhere around two years. When they finally arrived in Bethlehem, the scriptures tell us: *"On coming to the house, they saw the child with his mother Mary, and they bowed down and worshiped him"* (Matthew 2:11, NIV).

The truth is that wise men, and wise women, still need to know how and when to bow down and worship. In the Bible, bowing down or kneeling is a prominent worship posture. Between two Hebrew words—*bârak* (appearing 289 times) and *shakkah* (appearing 170 times)—kneeling or bowing before God is mentioned over 450 times. In no instance, however, does God tell us to bow down to him. He tells us never to bow down to another god, but never does he tell us to bow down before him. Perhaps God believes that when we come to know who he is and all he has done for us, we will choose to bow down. It will be the natural thing to do.

As you may remember from the story of Jesus's birth told in the book of Matthew, the Wise Men almost didn't make it to Bethlehem. They followed the star to Jerusalem, the capital city of Judah, with the tiny town of Bethlehem just a stone's throw away—less than five miles. But then the star disappeared. So they inquired of King Herod, thinking the current king of the Jews would know the whereabouts of the newborn king of the Jews. But, truth be told, Herod was exceedingly threatened by it, so much so that he devised a plan to eliminate this child. Terminate his life. Once Herod discerned where the child was born, he issued a mandate that all male children age two and under, who lived in and around Bethlehem, were to be killed.

Herod was insecure, paranoid, and obsessed with being the only king acknowledged by the Jews. He would do anything in his power to destroy any risk to his authority. There are still "Herods," today who come between us and worshiping God. Sometimes the "Herods" are insecure, power-obsessed persons. But mostly, they are unwelcome interruptions in life—the unexpected events that set us back or take us off-track from following our dreams; the disappointments and challenges, the struggles and losses that feel like raging

45

storms. And when they appear uninvited in our lives, it can feel like the rug has been pulled out from underneath every part of our existence. It can affect our emotions, our attitude, our family, our work, and yes, even our relationship with God.

The storms of life threaten our worship.

If there was ever a person who struggled with storms in their life, it was Job. Job was one of the most prominent men of his day. He was powerful. He was rich. And he was also deeply religious. The Bible says he was the most righteous man of his day. But he wasn't above being attacked by the Enemy. In fact, in one day, Satan destroyed almost everything near and dear to him: 500 yoke of oxen and 500 donkeys, 7,000 sheep and 3,000 camels, all his servants, and even his seven sons and three daughters. The Bible says, *"Job arose, tore his clothes, shaved his head, fell to the ground, and worshipped. He said: 'Naked I came from my mother's womb; naked I will return there. The Lord has given; the Lord has taken; bless the Lord's name'"* (Job 1:20-21).

Wouldn't you like to have that kind of faith, that kind of mindset? What was it that made Job so steadfast in his relationship with God? Was he superhuman? Or did he just know a couple of things that we could learn, so that when the storms of life come, we'd know that we could run to God, and even learn, as the Casting Crowns song says, to "praise you in this storm." The key is to know how to pour out our heart in a healthy way, in a way that leads toward God instead of away from him. Here are four keys to pouring out our heart in worship.

1. Seek God as Our Refuge.

A refuge is a safe place. Sometimes children have a safe place, somewhere to go if things are bad. Sometimes a safe place can be a person, like when a child is scared and runs into their daddy's arms. In the Bible, some of those who were closest to God knew him as that kind of heavenly Father. When the storms of life hit, they turned to him. One such person was David. In Psalm 62:5-8, he writes, *"Oh, I must find rest in God only, because my hope comes from him! Only God is my rock and my salvation—my stronghold!—I will not be shaken. My deliverance and glory depend on God. God is my strong rock. My refuge is in God. All you people: Trust in him at all times! Pour out your hearts before him! God is our refuge!"*

2. Pour Out What Is Truly in Our Hearts.

But what if there is nothing but darkness in our hearts? What if we are angry, bitter, disappointed, or full of doubt? Yes, bring that to God. C. S. Lewis once wrote, "We should bring to God what is in us, not what ought to be in us." You see, the "oughts" will keep us from telling the truth. The "oughts" will also keep us from feeling the truth, especially the truth about our pain.

God already knows what is in our heart. We cannot hide it from him. There is no pretending. We can do that with others, but not with God. In Psalm 142, David writes, *"I cry out loud for help from the Lord. I beg out loud for mercy from the Lord. I pour out my concerns before God; I announce my distress to him. . . . I cry to you, Lord, for help. 'You are my refuge,' I say. 'You are all I have in the land of the living'"* (Psalm 142:1-2, 5).

Do you have a complaint? God can handle it. Angry at someone? God has dealt with that before. In trouble? You can tell God. When the storms of life hit and when the Enemy tries to destroy all that is near and dear to us, we can go one of two ways. We can turn away from God and blame him, growing more isolated and bitter by the day. Or we can turn toward God, seeking him as our refuge, pouring out what is truly in our heart. And as we pour out our heart to God, our pain is transformed into praise.

3. Remember God's Faithfulness in the Past.

One of the most prominent prophets in the Old Testament was a man named Jeremiah. He wrote two books of the Old Testament—the one named after him, and the book of Lamentations. Laments are passionate expressions of grief or sorrow. Jeremiah knew what it was like to feel isolated and alone, rejected by the people around him. Yet look at what he writes: *"I called on your name, Lord, from the depths of the pit. You heard my plea. . . . You came near when I called you, and you said, 'Do not fear.' You, Lord, took up my case; you redeemed my life"* (Lamentations 3:55-58, NIV).

4. Trust in God's Promises and Power for the Future.

Recall in the story of Jesus's birth when the angel appeared to Joseph and told him to take Mary and baby Jesus to Egypt. God had been faithful in the past. God had provided Jesus a home in Bethlehem, and then, with the arrival of the Wise Men, gifts of gold, frankincense, and myrrh.

Likewise, God has a plan and purpose for our lives as well. Even though the Herods, the storms of life, seem threatening, God's power is greater, and his will *will* be done! It is like the prophet Jeremiah wrote, a truth many of us have memorized and hold onto in the midst of the storms: *"The Lord proclaims: When Babylon's seventy years are up, I will come and fulfill my gracious promise to bring you back to this place. I know the plans I have in mind for you, declares the Lord; they are plans for peace, not disaster, to give you a future filled with hope"* (Jeremiah 29:10-11).

God desires and deserves our worship. We have been created to worship God. Worship is not just a certain hour once a week, or a style of music. It is our expression or praise and honor to our heavenly Father. While this worship may be reverent, it may also include us singing loudly, raising our hands, or bowing on our knees. The style of our worship is not what is ultimately important to God—just that it is directed to him. So seek God as a refuge, pour out what is truly in your heart, remember God's faithfulness in the past, and trust in God's promises and power for the future.

Group Discussion Questions

1. What comes to mind when you hear the word *worship*? How have you seen the word *worship* used in the church?

2. What types of challenges tend to keep you from truly worshiping God with all your heart?

3. What would it look like for you to grow in this spiritual discipline?

4. How can this group best help you on your journey?

5. Which part of our session today spoke to you the most? Why?

6. How have you experienced God in your life this week?

Chapter 7
SPIRITUAL DISCIPLINE OF SABBATH

Remember the Sabbath day and treat it as holy. Six days you may work and do all your tasks, but the seventh day is a Sabbath to the LORD your God. Do not do any work on it—not you, your sons or daughters, your male or female servants, your animals, or the immigrant who is living with you. Because the LORD made the heavens and the earth, the sea, and everything that is in them in six days, but rested on the seventh day. That is why the LORD blessed the Sabbath day and made it holy.

– Exodus 20:8-11

Jesus went to Nazareth, where he had been raised. On the Sabbath he went to the synagogue as he normally did and stood up to read.

– Luke 4:16

If you stop trampling the Sabbath,
stop doing whatever you want on my holy day,
and consider the Sabbath a delight,
sacred to the LORD, honored,
and honor it instead of doing things your way,
seeking what you want and doing business as usual,
then you will take delight in the LORD.
I will let you ride on the heights of the earth;
I will sustain you with the heritage of your ancestor Jacob.
The mouth of the LORD has spoken.

– Isaiah 58:13-14

Remember "snow days" when you were a kid? While not every part of the country gets enough snow to close local schools, there are usually some types of weather that will cause administrators to close schools for the day. Many of us grew up in areas where the forecast of snow would cause us to watch TV all night, waiting to see our school listed on the news scroll at the bottom of the screen. Of course, it is not just children who love snow days. Most adults get excited about having a day off from work too. The weather is out of our control, so we feel this sense of relief being forced not to go to work. It's best when it is really bad because everyone else is playing by the same rules, so no one else is able to get ahead of us at work. We have a day to just unplug, disconnect, and relax.

Here's the good news: No matter what the weather forecast is this week, God has a snow day planned for us. And not just one snow day once in a while, but one every week of the year! God has even given these special weekly snow days a name: Sabbath.

Let's begin by taking a look at what scripture tells us about Sabbath. The first thing is this: God established and commanded Sabbath-keeping. Sabbath has its roots in creation. Sabbath was central and purposeful. God makes a point to create a seventh day, then purposefully do nothing on it. Genesis 2:2-3 reads: *"On the sixth day God completed all the work that he had done, and on the seventh day God rested from all the work that he had done. God blessed the seventh day and made it holy, because on it God rested from all the work of creation."*

God established Sabbath by creating it and then modeling its purpose: to cease from work and rest. That's the actual definition of *Sabbath*—to cease from work and rest. And what God established and exemplified, he then commanded us to follow his lead. The fourth of God's Ten Commandments given to the Hebrew people—people who had lived in slavery for hundreds of years and knew nothing but working seven days a week until they died—had to literally leave them awestruck. Instead of a taskmaster driving them with a whip to produce more and more bricks to build Pharaoh's latest pyramid, here was their God commanding them to take a day off. (Read Exodus 20:8-11 again.)

The word *holy* means "separate, set apart, sacred, different." Sabbath is not like the rest of the days of the week, where we are ON. Rather, it is permission to be OFF. Recently, the French passed a labor reform bill requesting companies with fifty or more employees to limit the spillover of work, specifically as it is related to "digital technology," into the private lives of employees. In doing so, they established a policy that specifies hours when employees are not to send or receive work emails. "All the studies show there is far more work-related stress today than there used to be, and that the stress is constant," Benoit Hamon of the French National Assembly told the BBC. "Employees physically leave the office, but they do not leave their work. They remain attached by a kind of electronic leash—like a dog. The texts, the messages, the emails—they colonize the life of the individual to the point where he or she eventually breaks down." This is exactly why God established and commanded his people to keep the Sabbath holy.

Sabbath is intended to save God's people. Work had enslaved them for centuries. Sabbath was, first, a demonstration that they were free people, and second, a way to keep them from breaking down. As Pete Scazzero, author of *Emotionally Healthy Spirituality* writes, "To keep Sabbath is to exercise one's freedom, to declare oneself to be neither a tool to be 'employed,' nor a beast to be burdened." There is a famous saying among the Jews, originally credited to Zionist writer Adad Ha'Am, which goes: "More than Jews have kept the Sabbath, the Sabbath has kept the Jews."

Sabbath is intended to save God's people; it is also intended to show God's power and grace. Pulling back from working is a statement of faith and trust in God's power to provide for us today, just as he provided for his people when they wandered in the wilderness for forty years without anything to eat. God provided something called manna, which fell on the Hebrew camp every single day for forty years. Every day, they could only get what they needed to eat that day, trusting that God would provide again the next day. If they succumbed to scarcity and gathered more than they needed, it would always rot by the second day. But there was one exception. Every Friday, they were commanded to gather twice as much so they didn't have to work on Saturday—their Sabbath. Miraculously, the Friday manna had a two-day shelf life! It was a sign to show God's people—and surrounding nations—that God

53

would provide. Exodus 31:13-14 reads: *"Tell the Israelites: 'Be sure to keep my sabbaths, because the Sabbath is a sign between me and you in every generation so you will know that I am the Lord who makes you holy. Keep the Sabbath, because it is holy for you.'"*

Getting a "snow day" in the Sinai Desert—yet growing stronger and stronger, multiplying and being blessed—was a sign that separated and differentiated God's people from all the other nations that surrounded them, cultures that operated seven days a week. It is a sign we belong to God, and also a means of God's grace. You see, Sabbath teaches us grace—that we are unconditionally loved by God apart from anything we do or produce. In her book *Sabbath Keeping*, Lynne Baab writes, "As long as we are working hard, using our gifts to serve others, experiencing joy in our work along with the toil, we are always in danger of believing our actions trigger God's love for us. Only in stopping, really stopping, do we teach our hearts and souls that we are loved apart from what we do."

God's Son, Jesus, said this: *"The Sabbath was made for man, not man for the Sabbath"* (Mark 2:27, NIV). Sadly, for many in Jesus's day, Sabbath had ceased to be a gift and had become another work of the Law—a legalistic way to earn God's love. There were thirty-nine categories of work that had to be avoided, everything from gathering and preparing food to mending clothes. Even writing or erasing two letters was prohibited!

What we see in scripture is that Jesus observed and clarified Sabbath-keeping. He clarified it by taking people back to the heart of Sabbath—not as a burden God was laying on his people, but rather a gift, a sign and means of his grace. Furthermore, while we see Jesus doing things on the Sabbath— things like healing people—that frequently got him in trouble with the Law-keeping zealots called Pharisees, the truth is that Jesus observed Sabbath. If anyone had the need and knew the power in ceasing work one day a week, it was Jesus! Luke 4:16 says that Jesus *"went to Nazareth, where he had been brought up, and on the Sabbath day he went into the synagogue, as was his custom"* (NIV).

For us, today, that may mean Sunday isn't our Sabbath. For many who work in the church, for example, Sunday isn't a day off. You may be employed in a place where you are required to work Sundays as well. Jesus would likely tell us the main thing is to establish the rhythm of one day off every seven, more than simply a set day of the week. Jews celebrate Friday at sunset until Saturday at sunset. Followers of Jesus started celebrating on Sundays. In 321, Emperor Constantine decreed Sunday instead of Saturday as a day of no work. Less important than a particular day of the week, it is the rhythm of one day off in seven.

Think back on the last time you were sick at home. Most of us have had the flu at one time or another. We end up drinking lots of fluids, eating some soup, and usually watching lots of TV from the couch. How many of those times we were sick, or maybe even hurt physically, was our body telling us we needed the rest? In his book *Sabbath*, Wayne Muller says, "If we do not allow for a rhythm of rest in our overly busy lives, illness becomes our Sabbath—our pneumonia, our cancer, our heart attack, our accidents create Sabbath for us." God created us to have a rest each week. Our bodies know that—and will react negatively when we are not giving them the rest they need.

Be careful not to let the legalistic perspective of Sabbath prevent you from seeing the beauty of what God wants for us. Yes, keeping the Sabbath is one of God's commandments. Like all good parents, our heavenly Father is giving us this rule because he wants the best for us. Failure to keep the Sabbath is not as much about punishment or condemnation as it is about missing out on the joy of resting in God's grace.

Like all of the spiritual disciplines we are covering in this study, the key is to think in terms of small steps. Be honest about where you are today in the discipline of Sabbath. Maybe you have never taken a real Sabbath. That's okay. Pick a day in the next week or two and try unplugging for a few hours. Work your way up to taking a Sabbath each week. Just don't listen to the voice in your head telling you it cannot be done, or you have too much to do to just sit and do nothing for a day. That is not God's voice. Pastor Eugene Peterson, author of The Message version of the Bible, writes, *"If you don't take a Sabbath, something is wrong. You're doing too much, you're being too much in charge. You've got to quit, one day a week, and just watch what God is doing when you're not doing anything."*

Here are three keys to enjoying the spiritual discipline of Sabbath:

55

1. Rest Your Body.

This is not about sitting on the couch all day and watching old movies. Resting your body may look different to each of us. Some may want to take a nap, others may rest by sitting under a tree and reading a good book, or maybe a long walk is rest to you. There is a story about a wagon train of Christians traveling on its way from St. Louis to Oregon. They observed the habit of stopping for the Sabbath during the autumn. But as winter approached, the group began to panic, fearing they wouldn't reach their destination before the snows began. Certain members of the group proposed they should quit stopping for the Sabbath and travel seven days a week, which caused an argument in the community. It was finally decided to divide the wagon train into two groups. One group would stop on the Sabbath day; the other would press on. Guess which group arrived in Oregon first? The ones who kept the Sabbath. You see, both the people and their horses were so rested by their Sabbath-keeping that they were able to work more efficiently the other six days.

2. Replenish Yourself.

What is it that fills your bucket? Life can be draining. The Sabbath is a day to be replenished. Try making a list of all the things that bring you joy and make you feel ready to take on the world. Then each Sabbath, do at least one of the things on your list.

3. Restore Your Soul.

Spend time in worship. Read a story in the Bible and really listen for God to speak to you. Try being quiet for a while. Serve someone.

As we end this session on Sabbath, take a minute now to read and reflect on the poem "Fire" by Judy Brown. Notice the importance of "space" and how that might connect to the need for a Sabbath in your own life.

Fire

What makes a fire burn is space between the logs, a breathing space.

Too much of a good thing, too many logs packed in too tight can douse
the flames almost as surely as a pail of water would.

So building fires requires attention to the spaces in between, as much as
to the wood.

When we are able to build open spaces in the same way we have learned
to pile on logs, then we can come to see how it is fuel, and absence of
the fuel together, that make fire possible.

We only need lay a log lightly from time to time.

A fire grows simply because the space is there, with openings in which
the flame that knows just how it wants to burn can find its way.

Group Discussion Questions

1. What has been your understanding of the Sabbath? How do you feel you have done at honoring the Sabbath?

2. What obstacles will need to be addressed for you to be able to truly observe the Sabbath?

3. What would it look like to take a small step in this spiritual discipline in the next season of your life?

4. How can this group best help you on your journey?

5. Which part of our session today spoke to you the most? Why?

6. How have you experienced God in your life this week?

Chapter 8

SPIRITUAL DISCIPLINE
OF COMMUNITY

*In the same way, though there are many of us, we are one body in Christ,
and individually we belong to each other.*

– Romans 12:5

*Love should be shown without pretending. Hate evil, and hold on to what is good. Love
each other like the members of your family. Be the best at showing honor to each other.
Don't hesitate to be enthusiastic—be on fire in the Spirit as you serve the Lord! Be happy
in your hope, stand your ground when you're in trouble, and devote yourselves to prayer.
Contribute to the needs of God's people, and welcome strangers into your home. Bless
people who harass you—bless and don't curse them. Be happy with those who are happy,
and cry with those who are crying. Consider everyone as equal, and don't think that
you're better than anyone else. Instead, associate with people who have no status. Don't
think that you're so smart. Don't pay back anyone for their evil actions with evil actions,
but show respect for what everyone else believes is good. If possible,
to the best of your ability, live at peace with all people.*

– Romans 12:9-18

Whatcomes to mind when you hear the term *social media*? People
have been communicating over great distances for hundreds of
years. What we think of as postal services date back to five hundred years
before Christ. The telegraph was invented in 1792; the telephone in 1890;

and radio in 1891. Everything really changed in the late twentieth century with the invention of computers. The first e-mail was sent in 1971. What we think of today as social media traces back to Friendster in 2002, which grew to over one hundred million users by 2008. As of this writing, some of the most popular social media sites are LinkedIn, Twitter, Instagram, and Pinterest. The largest is Facebook, with over two billion users worldwide.

Even if you have never sent a tweet, or friended someone on Facebook, or connected to someone on LinkedIn, the social media world is here to stay, and it is having an impact on our culture, our families, our children, and our grandchildren. As followers of Jesus Christ, we are called to engage our culture. We have a responsibility to add our voice to the conversation. We need to be informed enough to talk intelligibly and to ask questions that cause people to pause and reflect on the decisions they are making, on the ways they are using social media and integrating it into their lives. Because while there are some very cool features and advantages to being a part of the virtual world, there are also some pitfalls. Like the Internet and all forms of technology, it is how we use them that determines their value.

Just to state the obvious: social networking and social media are both intended to be social. In other words, these are places where people can connect with each other, develop relationships, and share their lives with one another in such a way that virtually eliminates the boundaries of time and space. You can have near-instant conversations and community with people around the corner as well as halfway around the world.

The genesis of all social media/networking sites is often attributed to Classmates.com and the crazy idea that people actually wanted to reconnect with people they had gone to school with. All it took was for the World Wide Web to make the jump from 1.0 to 2.0—from a passive place where users could strictly post and access information, to a dynamic medium where users could actually interact with one another. It was an instant hit. Why? Because it tapped into one of our fundamental needs as human beings: relationships. Connecting to others. The Bible says that we are created to do life together. We are created for community. Just as our creator God exists as a relationship—a connected, Trinitarian community: Father, Son, and Holy Spirit—God never intended for us to do life alone.

Over four hundred years ago, English poet John Donne penned the words, "No man is an island entire of itself; every man is a piece of the continent, a part of the main." It is what God communicated in the days of creation. After creating Adam on the Sixth Day, the Bible tells us, *"Then the Lord God said, 'It's not good that the human is alone. I will make him a helper that is perfect for him'"* (Genesis 2:18).

The Apostle Paul writes this is Romans 12:5: *"In the same way, though there are many of us, we are one body in Christ, and individually we belong to each other."* Circle the word belong in the previous sentence. This is key. In marriage, the Bible tells us that our bodies don't belong solely to us, but to our spouse as well. The calling is for the two to become "one flesh." In covenant community, we belong to one another in such a way that we can come to count on and depend upon each other. The New Testament lists no fewer than forty times the words one another in describing the way we are called to do life together—the obligations and responsibilities of community.

And nowhere do we see this coming together of our intrinsic need for relationship coupled with the inherent responsibility to support and care for one another than in the words of Jesus himself, in what we remember today as the Great Commandment—not a suggestion, but a mandate to do life together. In Matthew 22:37-39, Jesus says, *"You must love the Lord your God with all your heart, with all your being, and with all your mind. This is the first and greatest commandment. And the second is like it: You must love your neighbor as you love yourself."*

Let's face it. Life is hard. It is full of challenges and setbacks. It is full of victories and defeats. As covenant community, we are told by the Apostle Paul in 1 Corinthians 12:25-27, *"so that there won't be division in the body...the parts might have mutual concern for each other. If one part suffers, all the parts suffer with it; if one part gets the glory, all the parts celebrate with it. You are the body of Christ and parts of each other."*

The question then become, does social networking provide a help or a hindrance? Is it an aid or an obstacle? Let's look first at some positives:

1. **Is open to everyone.** Young and old, rich and poor. All races and religions. It is truly a melting pot where every person has the

opportunity to be included and engaged. No membership fees for most sites. No need to prove yourself worthy to be a part. No classes to complete.

2. Provides a sense of belonging. Some people have trouble forming friendships. They may struggle with being accepted. They haven't found a church or club or organization that they feel like they fit into, or that their schedule will allow them to participate with. So social networking can certainly provide this human need.

3. Provides ability to keep in touch with friends and loved ones. The ability to share pictures and videos, thoughts and experiences are important to keeping relationships alive.

4. Possesses quick speed and breadth of communication. Suppose you have a family member who has a health crisis or some other emergency. Social media allows you to instantly send out a prayer concern to hundreds of people—a circle of "peeps" that may reach all around the world—in the middle of the night from a hospital room. For individuals, as well as organizations and communities like the church, social media certainly extends the reach and influence of community.

There are many more benefits and ways that social networking can contribute to our sense of community and doing life together, but now let's look at the other side, the potential negatives for us to be aware of:

1. Distracts us from the present moment. This is huge and creating all sorts of problems, from users updating their Facebook status and checking tweets during work hours to not being able to engage with family during mealtimes.

2. Robs face-to-face relationships. Have you ever been talking to a friend, having a real heart-to-heart conversation, and a beep goes off on their phone and they tell you to "hold on just a minute"?

3. Gives a false sense of belonging. As much as social media can create a sense of belonging, you have to wonder how genuine and authentic that really is. Just because someone gets added to a list or circle of friends and is able to post comments on other people's "wall," does this constitute belonging?

4. **Has a lack of accountability.** This too is huge. Being in relationship with one another inherently brings responsibility. Users of social media—especially children and youth—are often unaware of the consequences of what they say and post. Do you realize that there is a permanent, non-erasable repository of posts and comments out there somewhere? Employers—current and future—can take a look at the pictures that get shared and the language that is chosen. And then there is the whole concept of cyberbullying and gossip, people saying things they wouldn't have the audacity or nerve to say face-to-face.

Again, this list is not intended to be exhaustive, but you get the idea. This is something that holds tremendous value and potential for us, but it is also something we have to engage with prudence. In the end, social networking is a supplement, not a substitute, for **community**. There are things that social networking adds that can certainly complement and enhance certain aspects of community. But alone, it is incomplete.

On one hand, social networking is interactive and user-convenient. It can be a huge advantage to be able to respond to others and have them respond to us. And it is also certainly advantageous, it would seem, to be able to do that whenever it is convenient to our schedules—that two people, or even a community of people, aren't limited to being able to connect on those rare occasions that works out for everyone.

But, on the other hand, biblical community is interdependent and covenantal. We need one another. Covenant carries a deeper sense of obligation and responsibility. It acknowledges the truth about life—that it isn't always as orderly and planned out as we'd prefer. And that means that community can be messy. It is not just about "interacting" when it is convenient and works out for us, but there are times when we show up because there is a great need for us to drop what we're doing and be fully present.

Biblical community takes us beyond simply "socializing." It takes us to the level of truly doing life together, sharing our story with others, learning trust and commitment and accountability, listening to one another with empathy, praying for each other, demonstrating compassion to one another, serving one another, and even sacrificing for, and suffering with, one another.

Biblical community is encompassed by the Greek New Testament word *koinonia* (New Testament fellowship): to be as committed to one another as we are to Jesus Christ.

> *Love should be shown without pretending. Hate evil, and hold on to what is good. Love each other like the members of your family. Be the best at showing honor to each other. Don't hesitate to be enthusiastic—be on fire in the Spirit as you serve the Lord! Be happy in your hope, stand your ground when you're in trouble, and devote yourselves to prayer. Contribute to the needs of God's people, and welcome strangers into your home. Bless people who harass you—bless and don't curse them. Be happy with those who are happy, and cry with those who are crying. Consider everyone as equal, and don't think that you're better than anyone else. Instead, associate with people who have no status. Don't think that you're so smart. Don't pay back anyone for their evil actions with evil actions, but show respect for what everyone else believes is good. If possible, to the best of your ability, live at peace with all people.* (Romans 12:9-18)

Here are several key elements to effective Christian communities:

- **Size**—A large group, twenty or more, is great for fellowship, and for listening to a speaker. A small group, twelve or so, (no matter what it is called, e.g., Sunday school, life group, etc.), is better for really doing life together.

- **Accountability**—As we grow together as followers of Christ, and begin to share our struggles and challenges with each other, we then have the opportunity to hold each other accountable, in a spirit of love, positively, with the desire to provide encouragement and support. Not negatively.

- **Congregational Care**—Our Christian community should be the first line of support for sickness, accidents, or other such needs.

- **Service**—Several times a year each group in the church should coordinate and execute service projects around the church and in the local community.

- **Fun**—Nothing brings a group together more than having fun together. Plan several times during the year to do something fun as a group.

The Son has called us into community—his community, the church—to share in the joys and struggles and even the messiness of life, not only when it is convenient and fits into our schedules, but when other have need. And as we live in this community, not only do other individuals have their needs met—and not only do we have our needs met—but most importantly, we grow into the image of Christ, and be part of his redemptive community that models a better, more complete picture of community in our world today.

Group Discussion Questions

1. What has been your experience with social media/networking? What do you like the best and least? How might our group learn from, or better utilize, social media? What boundaries might be helpful for our group?

2. What are we doing best as a Christian community? Where do we need to grow?

3. What step do you need to take in this spiritual discipline?

4. How can this group best help you on your journey?

5. Which part of our session today spoke to you the most? Why?

6. How have you experienced God in your life this week?

Chapter 9
SPIRITUAL DISCIPLINE
OF WITNESS

Jesus came near and spoke to them, "I've received all authority in heaven and on earth. Therefore, go and make disciples of all nations, baptizing them in the name of the Father and of the Son and of the Holy Spirit, teaching them to obey everything that I've commanded you. Look, I myself will be with you every day until the end of this present age."

– Matthew 28:18-20

But in your hearts revere Christ as Lord. Always be prepared to give an answer to everyone who asks you to give the reason for the hope that you have. But do this with gentleness and respect.

– 1 Peter 3:15, NIV

In Mark Twain's classic, *Huckleberry Finn*, Huck is the son of the town drunk, Pap. Huck is pretty much a homeless vagrant, until he is taken in by the Widow Douglas, who tries to redeem Huck from his directionless life. She educates him in academics and Christianity. Now both the Widow Douglas and her sister, Miss Watson, have good hearts and mean well, but they come off as the prototypical "Church Ladies"—pious, prudish, and judgmental. Here is how Huck describes the situation:

The widow's sister, Miss Watson, a tolerable slim old maid, with goggles on, had just come to live with her, and took a set at me now with a spelling-book. She worked me middling hard for about an hour, and then the widow made her ease up. I couldn't stood it much longer. Then for an hour it was deadly dull, and I was fidgety.

Miss Watson would say, "Don't put your feet up there, Huckleberry;" and "Don't scrunch up like that; Huckleberry, set up straight;" and pretty soon she would say, "Don't gap and stretch like that, Huckleberry; why don't you try to behave?"

Then she told me all about the bad place, and I said I wished I was there. She got mad then, but I didn't mean no harm.

All I wanted was to go somewhere; all I wanted was a change, I warn't particular. She said it was wicked to say what I said; said she wouldn't say it for the whole world; she was going to live so as to go to the good place. Well, I couldn't see no advantage to going where she was going, so I made up my mind I wouldn't try for it.

How often do you think this scene gets played out in our world today, where modern-day Hucks view Christians as uptight, self-righteous, judgmental sticks-in-the-mud? Do unchurched people look at the lives of "Christians," as a whole, and leave unimpressed, not feeling compelled to know more? Let's face it: It does not appear as though they are lining up, beating down the doors of the church to get in and discover Christianity for themselves. If heaven—"the good place"—is what we are living for, how many people around us would say, like Huck, "Well, I couldn't see no advantage in going where she was going, so I made up my mind I wouldn't try for it"?

As Christians, we are called to be *winsome*—defined as "attractive or appealing in appearance or character." This is the exact opposite of Huck's description of the Widow Douglas and Miss Watson. Our goal is to become more aware of our influence and opportunity with our friends and family who don't know Jesus, or do not have a church home. The more we practice being winsome, the more occasions we will have to *win some* to Jesus.

Pastor and author Louie Giglio offers four irresistible attributes of attractive Christian character:

1. Extravagant in a stingy world.

2. Kind in a self-centered world.

3. Faithful in a fickle world.

4. Secure in an insecure world.

How those who are unchurched see us, our character, is very important. At some point, it will lead them to ask us why we are how we are. They will notice what is different about us. Have you ever wondered what to say to a co-worker or neighbor who questions why you attend church or believe in God? Have you ever tried to hide your belief or faith from others, out of fear for being asked about something you did not feel equipped to talk about? There is good news! There is a simple, but fail-safe method that cannot be denied. It is what Louie Giglio calls the "irrefutable argument," which is an interesting way of saying it, because the "irrefutable, undeniable argument" is not really an "argument" at all. The one thing no one can argue about is our story. What difference has God made in your life? That story is your "irrefutable argument" because there is no other side to that story.

Will Rogers once said, "People's minds are changed through observation and not through argument." There is a lot of truth in that. Seeing is believing. Seeing something with our own eyes being played out right in front of us is a lot more convincing than hearing even the most logical, rational explanation. When it comes to hearing even the most airtight of arguments, there is still something inside of us that hesitates to fully embrace the point. But there is no arguing when we observe the truth firsthand.

This is especially true when it comes to sharing something as personal as our faith, something the most brilliant scientist and philosophers and theologians have argued about for thousands of years. Hundreds of books have been written on all sides of the issues of faith. The main reason these do not convince everyone to follow Jesus is that arguments are not winsome! Think about it. When we get into an argument with someone, the tendency is to get upset and angry. We get defensive. We don't even really listen to what the other person is saying, because all we are concerned about is being right and winning the argument. Not very helpful.

What does scripture tell us about living a winsome life? Let's take a look at what the Apostle Paul says:

Though I am free and belong to no one, I have made myself a slave to everyone, to win as many as possible. To the Jews I became like a Jew, to win the Jews. To those under the law I became like one under the law (though I myself am not under the law), so as to win those under the law. To those not having the law I became like one not having the law (though I am not free from God's law but am under Christ's law), so as to win those not having the law. To the weak I became weak, to win the weak. I have become all things to all people so that by all possible means I might save some. I do all this for the sake of the gospel, that I may share in its blessings. (1 Corinthians 9:19-23, NIV)

This message is expressed very well in the New Living Translation where we read: *"I try to find common ground with everyone, doing everything I can to save some. I do everything to spread the Good News and share in its blessings"* (vv. 22-23).

Our main verse for this session is from the Apostle Peter, who urges us:

But in your hearts revere Christ as Lord. Always be prepared to give an answer to everyone who asks you to give the reason for the hope that you have. But do this with gentleness and respect, keeping a clear conscience, so that those who speak maliciously against your good behavior in Christ may be ashamed of their slander. (1 Peter 3:15-16, NIV)

As followers of Jesus, we are called to live winsomely in front of others. Eventually, this will evoke questions, questions we are supposed to be prepared to answer. The reason for the hope we have in God is our irrefutable experience. It is our life. Our story. It is not something we have to enroll in seminary and take classes to learn. It is not a series of seven steps we need to follow, or a systematic theology of six scripture verses to share with others. It is our personal walk with Christ. What difference has knowing and following Jesus made in our lives? All believers are a story of amazing grace.

"Amazing Grace," possibly the most beloved hymn of our faith, was written by John Newton. It is the story of his conversion. Newton grew up with no church experience. He did not believe in God. He was pressed into service in the English Royal Navy. After he got out, he used his naval experience to get into the slave-trade business. He gained notoriety as the most foul-mouthed and profane sailor on his ship.

During a horrible storm that destroyed his boat, Newton made a promise to God. If God saved him, then Newton would become a new man. God did save Newton—not just from the storm, but from the eternal consequences of his sin. Newton began studying scripture, attended seminary, and was eventually ordained in the Church of England. He wrote "Amazing Grace" as an illustration for his sermon on New Year's Day 1773.

Amazing Grace, how sweet the sound,
That saved a wretch like me...
I once was lost but now am found,
Was blind, but now I see.

That is true for all of us! There was a time when all of us were "blind." We thought we could do life on our own. We did not need God, or we thought that there was no way God wanted or needed us...that we'd been too sinful...made too many bad decisions. But just like John Newton, when we open our heart to God, Jesus washes away our sin with his amazing grace, and the Holy Spirit begins to fill our lives, and we begin to change.

All believers are a story of amazing grace, and all believers are ambassadors of their story. We are a story of grace, and God calls all of us to share that story with others. Otherwise, God would not need to keep any of us here on earth. He'd just beam us up to heaven for eternity. We are here to tell others what God has done in our lives, the difference he has made, the change he's brought as we've put more and more trust in him.

In John 9, we read the story of Jesus's encounter with a man who'd been blind since his birth. Jesus spits on the ground, forms some mud, puts it on the man's eyes, and he is healed. Amazing grace! He was literally blind, but now could see. He goes home, and people begin to question him. He tells everyone what happened, but they do not believe him. The always-cynical Pharisees—who were great about telling people about how great God was but honestly didn't believe it, since they were always questioning Jesus's miracles—start questioning the man and calling Jesus a sinner. Then we read:

75

Therefore, they called a second time for the man who had been born blind and said to him, "Give glory to God. We know this man is a sinner." The man answered, "I don't know whether he's a sinner. Here's what I do know: I was blind but now I see." (John 9:24-25)

Look through the Gospels—the four accounts of Jesus's life in the New Testament—and you will see Jesus telling people he's healed to do the same thing. He doesn't send them home with scripture or a theological thesis on the nature of the Trinity. He says, "Just show them your life." We find a great example of this in the book of Mark. Jesus healed a man from Gerasene who was possess by a legion of demons:

While [Jesus] was climbing into the boat, the one who had been demon-possessed pleaded with Jesus to let him come along as one of his disciples. But Jesus wouldn't allow it. "Go home to your own people," Jesus said, "and tell them what the Lord has done for you and how he has shown you mercy." The man went away and began to proclaim in the Ten Cities all that Jesus had done for him, and everyone was amazed. (Mark 5:18-20)

As we become winsome, others will inquire about the "reason for the hope we have," so we must be prepared to give an answer, the irrefutable argument of our one and only life, our story of grace. Here are four keys to guide us:

1. **Identify the changes in our lives.** What difference has knowing Jesus and following him made in our lives? It does not need to be a story worthy of a Hollywood film or church song, but there does need to be a change—or else we may need to examine the truth of our relationship with Jesus.

2. **Trust that our story is perfect for us.** God has given each of us the story we need to tell to the people he will bring into our lives. There is a tendency to undersell the power of our own story; this often comes from comparing our story to the story God has given to other people. Each story is unique and exactly what is needed for us to share.

3. **Identify our fishing pond**. Jesus said to his disciples, *"Come, follow me… and I'll show you how to fish for people"* (Matthew 4:19). Too often we think we think of evangelism only in terms of sharing Jesus with complete strangers. While some of us may be called to do that, most of us need to focus closer to home. Our personal fishing pond should start with those we know the best (immediate family, close friends, neighbors, etc.) and then work outward to co-workers and acquaintances.

4. **Share our story and surrender the outcome to God.** Not many of us will share our story with a friend or neighbor, and then bow together in prayer, where the person we've shared with confesses their sin, accepts the amazing grace of Jesus, and asks the Holy Spirit to fill their life. Not that this cannot happen… just that it usually doesn't happen that way. More times than not, our story is going to be a "seed" that God uses, one bead in a series of stories, events, illustrations, and experiences to eventually lead someone to open their hearts to his love. And when and if God blesses us with the opportunity to be present when a friend or neighbor comes to faith, it is important that we stay humble and realize it probably wasn't all about us. There were probably others who had poured into that person's life, made deposits, and planted seeds along the way, and we were just fortunate enough to be in the right place at the right time.

That is why it is so important for us to share our story—because every seed matters. Every second someone lives apart from God, they're missing out on the amazing grace of Jesus, the abundant and eternal life he came to offer. We have all been healed and saved from a life of sin so that we can share that story of healing and grace with others.

Group Discussion Questions

1. What has changed in your life as a result of following Jesus? What differences might someone have noticed if they had known you for many years?

2. What has been your experience with discussing issues of faith or religion with others (especially the unchurched)?

3. Who in your "fishing pond" is God calling you to reach? What would be a first step?

4. How can this group best help you on your journey?

5. Which part of our session today spoke to you the most? Why?

6. How have you experienced God in your life this week?

SPIRITUAL DISCIPLINE OF PRESENCE

I tell you that you are Peter. And I'll build my church on this rock. The gates of the underworld won't be able to stand against it.

— Matthew 16:18

We have many parts in one body, but the parts don't all have the same function. In the same way, though there are many of us, we are one body in Christ, and individually we belong to each other.

— Romans 12:4-5

And let us consider each other carefully for the purpose of sparking love and good deeds. Don't stop meeting together with other believers, which some people have gotten into the habit of doing. Instead, encourage each other, especially as you see the day drawing near.

— Hebrews 10:24-25

Imagine you are on an airplane. You strike up a conversation with the person seated next to you, and he tells you he is a professional athlete. When you ask him what sport, he shares that he is a player on your favorite baseball team! But you don't recognize him....Maybe it is because he is not wearing a uniform. So you ask how long he has been on the team, and what position he plays. He replies, "Oh, I don't believe in playing on a team. I go solo with the baseball thing." How is that possible? Baseball is a team sport, right? There are certainly drills an individual can do, but baseball is designed to be played as a team.

This same contradiction is played out every week in our communities. How can a person say, "I'm a Christian, but I don't believe in the church"? Unfortunately, we are hearing that statement more and more today from people who claim to be "spiritual" people. And yet, here is the irony: that concept is completely inconsistent with the Bible. God never intended for us to live out our faith or work out our salvation in private. Christianity is not an individual activity; it is a team sport. The very idea of Lone Ranger Christianity is as crazy as playing baseball without a team.

Christianity must be personal, but it cannot be private. Jesus summed it up best when He said that Christianity was essentially *"loving God with all our heart, soul, mind, and strength; and loving our neighbor as we love ourselves"* (cf. Matthew 22:37-40). Christianity must be personal—a relationship I spend time nurturing with God through Bible study, prayer, and meditation. But it cannot end there. To be complete, the Christian life must be lived out in community. There is something essential about being in relationship with others who will both bless us and frustrate us, both of which are required to grow and shape us into God's people.

That is why God gave us his church—to be that community of faith. In the Old Testament, the community of faith was the people of Israel. In the New Testament, it is the church. In this session, we will discover why it is still the vehicle God uses to provide for our own spiritual needs, as well as to be his light to the world.

"I love Jesus, but not his church." Have you ever heard anyone say something like that? The irony is that in a time when "spirituality" seems to be soaring and at all-time highs, church participation is plummeting. Thousands of churches close their doors for the last time every year. While there are exceptions, many churches around the United States have not seen any real growth in attendance for years.

Why? Why do people today seem to have a "take it or leave it" attitude about the church? Why don't they feel compelled to be connected to, and part of, a local church community on a consistent basis? Here are a few of the more popular comments. See if any of these sound familiar:

- **"I'm too busy."**—This is the biggest issue in our culture today: busyness. We have become a 24/7 people. Sabbath is no longer sacred. When many of us were growing up, the only things open on Sundays were restaurants and gas stations. Attending church and worshiping God were considered priorities. Now, Sunday is just another day of the week. Our kids play sports. We run marathons, sleep in, or work around the house. The truth is that, regardless of how busy we become, we always make time for the things that really matter to us. And busyness has become a little less responsible way for people to say, "It's just not a priority for me."

- **"Church is full of hypocrites."**—Who hasn't heard of some church member or pastor who's always talking about God and offering platitude-laden advice and "spiritual truth" to others, only to get caught embezzling money or committing adultery? And who wants to hang out with a bunch of people who claim to believe in something on Sunday, then live completely differently the rest of the week? (It's nearly as bad as claiming to be a Christian but disowning the church.)

- **"Church just wants my money."**—For many, is seems like this is all the church is really after. The mission is the "bottom line" of the budget. It is not about helping people connect to God and grow in their faith. Instead, church is just one big "dog and pony show" that uses God to manipulate folks to give their hard-earned money to keep the institution going... wondering how the church plans to use that money to truly make a difference in the community and world.

- **"Church is irrelevant to my life."**—They have attended church in the past, but it was an exercise of boredom. The songs felt like they came out of another world, and the Bible wasn't explained or applied in any tangible way that had anything to do with the issues they were dealing with in their life.

- **"Church makes me feel guilty."**—Many people feel like church is a bunch of smug, self-righteous people who want to parade around their perfection. They use a lot of "us" and "them" language to put distance between the "good" and the "bad." As a result, imperfect people leave feeling even worse about themselves and their future than when they arrived.

- **"Church doesn't measure up to my spiritual standards."**—These are individuals who have very clear expectations for what the church should and should not be and what it should and should not do.

Their ideals are so high that no church can possibly meet their standards. In their Bibles, they carry detailed lists of the "right" ways to interpret scripture and apply doctrine. They have a lengthy list of what's "wrong" with each church in town:

- "The worship music isn't 'Spirit-led' enough."

- "The sermons are too shallow and don't 'feed me' anymore."

- The church is either too soft on sin, or it's too judgmental.

- The missions programs aren't aggressive enough, or it's all the church talks about.

- They spend way too much time and energy on building facilities; or they don't ever build space for my preferred program.

Churches, with our mere mortals, can never measure up.

- **"I can resource my own spiritual journey."**—The truth is, with all the resources available online and at our favorite local Christian bookstore, we can surround ourselves with all the Bible studies, sermon series, and daily devotionals we need. We can find ways to get involved in our community and serve others. We can give ten percent of our income to local and international charities. We can even share our faith with others. We can be the epitome of the American Christian—independent and able to pull ourselves up by our own spiritual bootstraps and become fully self-sanctified apart from formal religion.

If that last one is you…congratulations! Well done! It would be wonderful if all of us could mature to the point where we are spiritual self-feeders, where we don't need the church to hold our hand and teach us to feed ourselves. However, not everyone is there yet. Truth be told, there was a season in all of our lives where we did not have it all together and figured out, when we needed the church to live up to the vows she took when we were baptized, surround us with a community of love and grace, help us learn God's word, discover God's purpose for our life, and walk with us on those initial steps.

Even if we have matured to the point of being spiritual self-feeders, we still need the church.

Airplane pilots, when they are flying a route, are always giving and receiving information. They're getting important information about weather, storms, and turbulence from the pilot in the plane who's flying that route ahead of them. That helps them when they get to that same point on the route. Likewise, they're passing along conditions and other important information to the pilot flying fifteen minutes behind them. As the church, we need one another— Christians who are going before us to give us instruction, and Christians who are growing up behind us, so that we can share in the joy of helping them.

The problem with our personalized faith is that we can develop a consumer mentality when it comes to the church: that the church exists to bless me by feeding me more and more; preaching me sermons and providing me Bible studies to help me learn about God; offering children's programs where I can drop off my kids and expect them to be wowed by creativity and developed into fully devoted followers of Jesus...all in an hour a week; and on and on. And while that's spot-on truth, it's only half the story. The other half is that each one of us is the church. If God has led you to a local church, then not only does that church have something you need to take the next step in your spiritual journey, but you have something that local church needs to do a better job of representing Christ in the world. You see, the church isn't a building. The church isn't a program. We are the church. You are. All of us are. And as the church, we don't just exist for one another, but for the world as well. The church doesn't exist just for us, but also for the world.

As Bill Hybels, pastor at Willow Creek Community Church, has said time and again: "The local church is the hope of the world." We are the ones, called by God, to be his redemptive force in the world, calling people out of darkness and into his glorious light. In the New Testament, the original Greek word for church is *ekklesia*, which means "an assembly of called-out people." First Peter 2:9 says, *"But you are a chosen race, a royal priesthood, a holy nation, a people who are God's own possession. You have become this people so that you may speak of the wonderful acts of the one who called you out of darkness into his amazing light."*

The body of Christ is called and set apart by God for the purpose of declaring God's love and amazing grace, living beyond themselves, and radically loving not only one another, but the least and the last and the lost—the cast-outs and rejects, the imperfect people of each generation who are looking for acceptance, meaning, and purpose.

There are many great examples in the Bible, but one stands out. On the birthday of the church, the Day of Pentecost, just as Jesus prophesied, the Holy Spirit descended on the apostles like tongues of fire and filled them with the very power that filled Jesus during his earthly ministry. Acts 2:42-47 says,

> *The believers devoted themselves to the apostles' teaching, to the community, to their shared meals, and to their prayers. A sense of awe came over everyone. God performed many wonders and signs through the apostles. All the believers were united and shared everything. They would sell pieces of property and possessions and distribute the proceeds to everyone who needed them. Every day, they met together in the temple and ate in their homes. They shared food with gladness and simplicity. They praised God and demonstrated God's goodness to everyone. The Lord added daily to the community those who were being saved.*

The church—the people of God, the followers of Christ, filled with the power of the Holy Spirit—was, and is, the hope of the world. Let's take a quick look at what the New Testament tells us are Christ's purposes for his church:

1. ***Kerygma***—Share the good news. The church is called to preach and teach—to declare to one another and to declare to the world that God, in Christ, has defeated sin and death, and has offered us life abundant and eternal. The word *proclamation* is at the heart of *kerygma*. Romans 10:17 says, *"So, faith comes from listening, but it's listening by means of Christ's message."*

2. ***Leitorgia***—Celebrate the sacraments (baptism and Holy Communion). Sacraments are signs and means of God's grace. They are not ordinary acts. They are channels of divine revelation—how God meets us right where we are and helps us take next steps on our spiritual journey. Sacraments remind us of the faithfulness God has to the sacred covenant he has with his people. Sacraments are not private; they are communal experiences, reminding us of our God-given calling to do life together and to be responsible for one another.

3. ***Diakonia***—Serve the world. God has given each one of us at least one spiritual gift, which is used to connect us to the body of Christ and to help it grow and be all that it can be. Even beyond the church, Christ calls us to lay down our lives, just as he did, in service to those on the margins of life. That leads us to the fourth and final purpose....

4. ***Koinonia***—Spread kingdom community. The church often talks about "fellowship." Great word. But the New Testament meaning goes way beyond potluck dinners and hanging out at one another's house. *Koinonia* was a radical way of being—reaching out to include all the rejects of the ancient world. Slaves, women, the poor, sick, weak, elderly, infants, widows, and orphans were all drawn in and dignified. In a world that treated them as nobodies, the church accepted them as equals. It is what led to the world looking at the church in action and saying, "Look at how those Christians love one another!"

The church is a place where...

- the mature nurture the immature

- the healthy heal the unhealthy

- the loveable love the unlovable

- and the acceptable accept the unacceptable

We need God, and we need one another. Hebrews 10:24-25 says, *"And let us consider each other carefully for the purpose of sparking love and good deeds. Don't stop meeting together with other believers, which some people have gotten into the habit of doing. Instead, encourage each other, especially as you see the day drawing near."* We need one another. We need community. We need the church in order to be faithful to God's calling on our lives. Because while the Christian faith and experience must be personal, it cannot be private.

Group Discussion Questions

1. Which of the reasons people give for not going to church have you heard the most? What has been your response?

2. Over the years, what has been your main obstacle with attending church?

3. What would it look like for you to grow in this spiritual discipline?

4. How can this group best help you on your journey?

5. Which part of our session today spoke to you the most? Why?

6. How have you experienced God in your life this week?

CPSIA information can be obtained
at www.ICGtesting.com
Printed in the USA
LVHW03s0118230718
584379LV00001B/1/P

9 781501 876257